BERRIES

BERRIES

INTRODUCTION BY PEPITA ARIS

southwater

This edition is published by Southwater

Southwater is an imprint of
Anness Publishing Limited
Hermes House
88–89 Blackfriars Road
London SE1 8HA
tel. 020 7401 2077
fax 020 7633 9499

Distributed in the USA by
Anness Publishing Inc.
27 West 20th Street
Suite 504
New York
NY 10011
tel. 212 807 6739
fax 212 807 6813

Distributed in the UK by
The Manning Partnership
251–253 London Road East
Batheaston
Bath BA1 7RL
tel. 01225 852 727
fax 01225 852 852

Distributed in Australia by
Sandstone Publishing
Unit 1
360 Norton Street
Leichhardt
New South Wales 2040
tel. 02 9560 7888
fax 02 9560 7488

1 3 5 7 9 10 8 6 4 2

Publisher Joanna Lorenz
Senior Cookery Editor Linda Fraser
Project Editor Anne Hildyard
Designer Lisa Tai
Illustrations Anna Koska
Photographers Karl Adamson, Edward Allwright, Steve Baxter, James Duncan,
John Freeman, Michelle Garrett, Amanda Heywood and Michael Michaels
Recipes Carla Capalbo, Carole Clements, Elizabeth Wolf-Cohen, Roz Denny, Christine
France, Sarah Gates, Shirley Gill, Norma MacMillan, Katherine Richmond, Liz Trigg,
Laura Washburn and Steven Wheeler
Food for photography Elizabeth Wolf-Cohen, Marilyn Forbes, Cara Hobday, Wendy Lee,
Jane Stevenson and Liz Trigg
Stylists Madeleine Brehaut, Hilary Guy, Blake Minton and Kirsty Rawlings

For all recipes, quantities are given in both metric and imperial measures and, where
appropriate, measures are also given in standard cups and spoons. Follow one set, but not a
mixture, because they are not interchangeable.

Previously published as *Cooking with Berries*

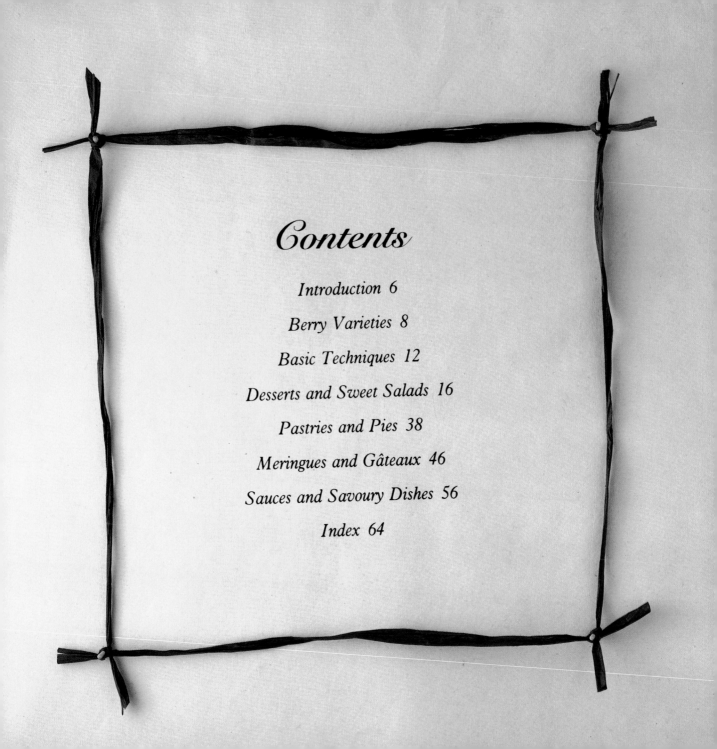

Contents

$\mathcal{I}$NTRODUCTION

Berries are the very essence of summer. The first sight of those bright colours in the shops inevitably conjures up thoughts of long, summer days, of picnics in the country and on the beach, of leisurely lunches and garden parties; and we long to begin eating just-picked fruit from a basket or even straight off the stem.

First among the berries to arrive are strawberries. Even though glass-grown strawberries are in the shops year-round, the first home-grown strawberries symbolize *par excellence* the arrival of summer sunshine. And strawberries are perfect for all summer occasions, whether it's a wedding breakfast, smart reception or just lunch for family and friends in the garden. Strawberries have a long history of delighting us: "Doubtless God could have invented a better berry" said a sixteenth-century aficionado "but doubtless he never did". In 1812, Dolly Madison, wife of the fourth US president and famous hostess, served strawberries picked from her own garden at the President's second Inaugural Ball at the White House. The first strawberries were tiny wild ones, like today's fraises des bois; the luscious monsters we now eat have been developed over the centuries.

Strawberries and raspberries both have their admirers. Perfection depends a little on the temperature zone you live in, as well as personal preference, though: strawberries need maximum sun but raspberries prefer a winter frost and a wetter climate.

Berries are, in essence, wild fruit – there is still a rich harvest, varying with the season: currants of all colours, blackberries, blueberries and bilberries, and even raspberries of different colours in North America. If you can't find wild fruits, you can always pick your own at farms that open for the purpose.

Don't forget the newer berries, either. A whole range has developed since Judge J H Logan first bred the loganberry in his garden in Santa Cruz, California. Tayberries, boysenberries, worcesterberries and jostas – the luscious names roll off the tongue.

The recipes in this book are divided into four sections. There's a helpful, information-packed introductory guide to varieties and choosing, preparing and cooking berries. The recipes begin with refreshing fruit salads, delicately scented soufflés, mousses and brightly coloured ices in the first chapter, pies and tarts bursting with juicy berries in the second, and gorgeous gâteaux and meringues in the third. They end in a selection of savoury ideas, including tangy raspberry vinaigrette, brilliant berry salsa, and classic cranberry sauce. This book will help you really make the most of the most luscious harvest of summer.

Berry Varieties

BLACKBERRY

Also called a bramble because it grows on bushes with thorns, the black-berry is a sweet, juicy black fruit made up of many tiny segments, each containing a tiny seed. Ripe berries can be eaten raw, but they are best after cooking, which softens the seeds and deepens the flavour. In the same family of plants, there are several varieties of a trailing type of blackberry, known as dewberries. Dewberries have a similar flavour to blackberries and are very juicy.

BLUEBERRY

This small, round, firm, purplish blue fruit is juicy and sweet, with a mild flavour, and is used in pies, jams and cheesecakes, or just eaten raw. Bilberries, which grow wild in many parts of Europe, are

members of the same family, but are much smaller and have a sharp, fragrant taste. These wild berries are called by many different names: blaeberry, whortleberry, hurtleberry and whinberry are just a few of the local variations. Bilberries are used for sauces to serve with game.

CRANBERRY

This smooth, bright red berry is very hard and sour, but once sweetened can be used in both sweet and savoury dishes. It makes an excellent piquant sauce to accompany poultry or to balance rich meats. Cranberries belong to the same plant family as the blueberry, and a natural berry, the cowberry, is yet another member that can be found in pastures and woodland. Another relative, the lingonberry, originally from Scandinavia, is a smaller version of

the cranberry, with the same tart flavour. Lingonberries can be used in any recipe which calls for cranberries.

CURRANTS

Blackcurrants and redcurrants are both small, tart berries which make wonderful jams, jellies and sauces

Raspberries

Blueberries

*Strawberry leaves
and flowers*

Blackberries

Strawberries

Redcurrants

to serve with meat and game dishes. The shiny, bright appearance of redcurrants also makes them an attractive addition to desserts.  Blackcurrants are best cooked and when sweetened have an intense tangy flavour. The rarer white currants are less tart and look delicate and pretty when used to decorate desserts and cakes.

HUCKLEBERRY

The huckleberry is a blue-black berry that resembles the blueberry in appearance, but the skin is thicker and the taste is more tart. Unlike the blueberry, which has tiny, soft seeds, the seeds in the centre are hard. They are good eaten plain or used in pies, tarts, jams and syrup. The tangleberry is a variety of huckleberry, found in North America, which grows near the sea. The berries are dark blue, with a sweet, piquant flavour. Their original name was dangleberry because they grow on very long stems.

RASPBERRIES

These deep red fruits are prized for their delicate flavour. Their soft texture means that they don't need cooking and they are popular as a decoration and filling for meringues and gâteaux. They can, of course, be cooked and make a wonderful filling for hot pies, especially when combined with apples. Crushed and sieved, they make a lovely fruity sauce to serve with ice cream or sorbet. As well as the classic red raspberry, white and yellow varieties are also grown, but are not widely available. A rarely cultivated type of raspberry is the Scandinavian cloudberry, a pink berry with a sweet taste. It is very delicate, hence it is not commercially grown. The salmonberry is a wild raspberry found in North America. The large berries are a salmon-pink colour, and they can be stewed or used instead of raspberries. The thimbleberry is a thimble-shaped, wild American flowering raspberry which is light red in colour and has a good flavour.

STRAWBERRY

A large, bright red fruit with an intense scented fragrance and a conical shape, the cultivated strawberry has been developed from crossbreeding a small wild American strawberry and a juicy variety from South America. Wild strawberries (fraises des bois) are also widely cultivated and are prized for their perfumed aroma. Strawberries are delicious served with cream or macerated in red wine, champagne or orange juice. They can be puréed to make a cold sauce or soup and can be cooked in dishes which only require short cooking, such as crème brûlée. Nowadays, strawberries are available all year round.

WINTERBERRY

This is the berry of the wintergreen, an evergreen herb native to North America. The plant retains its foliage throughout the whole winter, hence the name. The berries are bright red with a spicy taste, and make an attractive addition to puddings, pies, sauces and stuffings. They can be used in any recipe that calls for cranberries. Winterberries are sometimes known as checkerberries.

COUNTRY COUSINS

There are many new hybrids of blackberries and raspberries which have been developed to produce a number of interesting berries of varied size, colour and flavour.

BOYSENBERRY

These large, juicy berries are a hybrid of strawberries, raspberries, dewberries and loganberries. They look like very large, pale-fleshed blackberries and have a rich sweet-sour flavour.

LOGANBERRY

There is some controversy over the origin of this berry. The soft dark red berries are said to be a hybrid developed from wild blackberries in the UK and dewberries in the US, although others maintain that they are a raspberry-blackberry hybrid.

TAYBERRY

A hybrid of blackberries and raspberries, tayberries look like elongated raspberries but taste like ripe blackberries. They can be eaten raw, but like blackberries are best cooked.

YOUNGBERRY

Dewberries and loganberries were used in the development of this hybrid which is not yet widely cultivated. Youngberries are dark red, with a sweet, juicy flesh.

Basic Techniques

To strip redcurrants, blackcurrants and white currants from their stalks, pull the stalks through the tines of a fork to remove the berries.

To remove the green leafy top and central core from strawberries, use a special tool known as a "huller", or cut out the top and core with a knife.

Cooking Berries

• Place soft berries in a heavy-based pan and cook very gently for 3–5 minutes until just tender. Firmer berries will need up to 10 minutes.

• If you want to keep the fruits whole, add the sugar before cooking, cook over a very low heat and avoid stirring the fruits. Don't allow the berries to boil or they will break up.

To chop strawberries, remove the tops and cores and, using a small sharp knife, chop coarsely for salsas or desserts.

To macerate berries, place the fruit in a bowl, sprinkle with fruit liqueur, a spirit such as brandy or rum, or sugar or sugar syrup. This process allows the fruit to soften and absorb the liqueur.

12

COOK'S TIPS

● *Buying berries*: since berries are fragile and easily crushed, choose berries packed in small boxes or punnets. Look for bright colour and plump, firm flesh. Any leaves should be green and fresh.

● Home-grown berries are at their peak in the summer, although many fresh berries are now available all-year round imported from all over the world. Fresh cranberries have a short season in late autumn; frozen berries are available throughout the year.

● *Preparation*: most berries need very little cleaning: just remove tops and stalks where appropriate and discard any soft, mouldy or very unripe berries. Avoid washing them; a wipe with a piece of damp kitchen paper should suffice, so rinse the berries, especially the very soft ones, only if absolutely necessary.

● *Storing berries*: remove any mouldy or damaged berries, then either leave in the punnet or transfer to a shallow dish and cover loosely with clear film or kitchen paper. Berries are best eaten the day they are bought, however soft fruits can be chilled for up to 3 days (their scent diminishes after this) provided that they have not been rinsed first.

FREEZER TIPS

● Spread blueberries, cranberries, currants and raspberries on trays so the fruits are not touching and open freeze until firm. Pack the frozen berries in freezer bags or rigid plastic containers and return to the freezer until required.

● Sprinkle strawberries with sugar and pack into a rigid plastic container. The berries will yield some of their juice as they freeze which mixes with the sugar to produce a syrup and helps keep the berries firm and in good shape.

● Freeze whole berries for up to 1 year.

● Freeze puréed fruit with or without sugar for up to 6 months. Thaw for 2–3 hours at room temperature, or overnight in the fridge.

PERFECT PURÉES

Berries make vibrant and flavourful purées and sauces which are delicious poured over ice cream or served with desserts and cakes. A smooth sauce made from uncooked fruit purée is sometimes known as a coulis. Sauces and purées can be sweetened as much or as little as you like. Add a squeeze of lemon juice, or a little fruit liqueur, to accentuate and enhance the flavour. Use either fresh or frozen fruit for sauces. If using frozen berries, partially thaw them and drain on kitchen paper before puréeing.

To purée fresh berries, place them in a blender or food processor. Pulse the machine on and off a few times and scrape down the bowl to make sure all the berries are puréed.

To purée frozen berries, place in a saucepan with a little sugar and soften over a gentle heat to release the juices. Simmer for 5 minutes. Allow to cool.

Press the purée through a fine-mesh nylon sieve to remove any fibres and seeds. Add a little icing sugar, and either lemon juice or a fruit-flavoured liqueur, to taste.

QUICK DESSERT IDEAS

• Stir some coulis into whipped cream or yogurt for a quick marbled dessert.

• Pour a little coulis into individual serving dishes and turn out a mini fresh cream cheese on to each. Decorate with fresh berries.

• Stir a little coulis into seasonal mixed fruits to make a refreshing fruit salad. Berry coulis makes a healthy low-fat sauce; serve a spoonful or two with cakes, pastries, ice cream, or fruit desserts.

• Decorate desserts with fresh berries.

SIMPLE SAUCES

To make a pretty, feathered effect, use two fruit purées of contrasting colours, such as mango and raspberry. Pour a little of each on to a serving plate, then gently run a cocktail stick or skewer through several places where the sauces meet. Or, add drops of coulis to custard or other creamy sauces and use a cocktail stick or skewer to create a feathered pattern. Arrange sliced fruit over the sauces to decorate.

RASPBERRY COULIS WITH ICED MACAROON CREAM

A vibrant, tangy coulis is the perfect partner for this quick, elegant dessert.

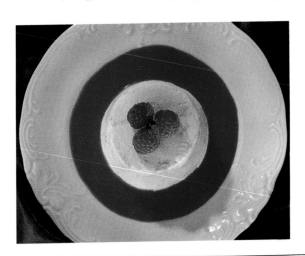

Whip 750ml/1¼ pints/3 cups whipping cream until it starts to thicken, then stir in 60ml/4 tbsp brandy or orange juice and 30ml/2 tbsp caster sugar and whip until the cream holds stiff peaks.

Fold in 115g/4oz coarsely crushed almond macaroons and spoon into six or eight ramekins. Cover and freeze until firm.

Unmould the desserts on to individual serving plates and leave for 5 minutes to soften slightly.

Pour a little raspberry coulis around the creams and serve, decorated with fresh raspberries.

Desserts and Sweet Salads

Summer berries bring a vibrant splash of colour to fresh fruit salads and compotes. Use them to delicately scent soufflés and mousses, and add a refreshing fruity flavour to ices and sauces.

SUMMER BERRY MEDLEY

Make the most of glorious berries in this refreshing dessert – just use whichever berries you have to hand.

Serves 4–6

175g/6oz/1½ cups redcurrants

175g/6oz/1 cup raspberries

50g/2oz/¼ cup caster sugar

30–45ml/2–3 tbsp crème de framboise
   or raspberry liqueur

450–675g/1–1½lb/3–5 cups mixed soft
   summer fruits, such as strawberries,
   raspberries, blueberries, redcurrants
   and blackcurrants

vanilla ice cream, to serve

VARIATION

*Instead of serving this summer
compote with ice cream add a
spoonful or two of thick Greek-
style yogurt, or swirl the fruit
mixture into 225g/8oz/1 cup
plain or strawberry-flavoured
fromage frais.*

Strip the redcurrants from their stalks using a fork and place them in a bowl with the raspberries, sugar and crème de framboise or raspberry liqueur. Cover and leave to macerate for 1–2 hours.

Put the fruit with its macerating juices in a pan and cook gently for 5–6 minutes, stirring occasionally, until the fruit is just tender.

Pour the fruit into a blender or food processor and blend until smooth. Press through a nylon sieve to remove any pips. Leave to cool, then chill.

Divide the mixed soft fruit among four individual glass serving dishes and pour over the sauce. Serve with scoops of vanilla ice cream.

SUMMER BERRY SALAD WITH FRESH MANGO SAUCE

When you have only a few berries to hand, combine them with other summer fruits to make a colourful, refreshing fruit salad. Serve it simply with cream or ice cream, or drizzle with a vibrant mango sauce.

Serves 6

1 large ripe mango, peeled, stoned and chopped

rind of 1 unwaxed orange

juice of 3 oranges

caster sugar, to taste

2 peaches

2 nectarines

1 small mango, peeled

2 plums

1 pear or 1/2 small melon

juice of 1 lemon

25–50g/1–2oz/2 heaped tbsp wild strawberries (optional)

25–50g/1–2oz/2 heaped tbsp raspberries

25–50g/1–2oz/2 heaped tbsp blueberries

small mint sprigs, to decorate

In a food processor fitted with the metal blade, process the large mango until smooth. Add the orange rind, juice and sugar to taste and process again until very smooth. Press through a sieve into a bowl and chill the sauce.

Peel the peaches, if liked, then slice and stone the peaches, nectarines, small mango and plums. Quarter the pear and remove the core and seeds, or, if using, slice the melon thinly and remove the peel.

Place the sliced fruits on a large plate, sprinkle the fruits with the lemon juice and chill, covered with clear film, for up to 3 hours before serving. (Some fruits may discolour if cut too far ahead of time.)

To serve, arrange the sliced fruits on serving plates, spoon the berries on top, drizzle with a little mango sauce and decorate with mint sprigs. Serve the remaining sauce separately.

STRAWBERRIES WITH COINTREAU

Strawberries are one of summer's greatest pleasures. Try this simple way to serve them.

Serves 4

1 unwaxed orange

40g/1½oz/3 tbsp granulated sugar

75ml/5 tbsp water

45ml/3 tbsp Cointreau or
orange liqueur

450g/1lb/3 cups strawberries, hulled

250ml/8fl oz/1 cup whipping cream

VARIATION

Instead of using strawberries on their own in this dessert, add a mixture of other fresh seasonal berries, such as raspberries and blueberries, along with sliced summer fruits like peaches and nectarines.

Peel wide strips of rind without the pith from the orange and cut into very thin julienne strips. Combine the sugar and water in a small saucepan. Bring to the boil over a high heat, swirling the pan occasionally to dissolve the sugar. Add the julienne strips and simmer for 10 minutes. Remove the pan from the heat and leave the syrup to cool, then stir in the Cointreau.

Reserve four strawberries for decoration and cut the rest in halves or quarters. Put them in a bowl and pour the syrup and orange rind over the top. Set aside for 2 hours. Whip the cream and sweeten to taste. Serve the strawberries with cream and the reserved strawberries.

PEACHES WITH RASPBERRY SAUCE

Escoffier created this dessert, known as Peach Melba, in honour of the opera singer Nellie Melba.

Serves 6

1 litre/1³/4 pints/4 cups water

50g/2oz/¹/4 cup caster sugar

1 vanilla pod, split lengthways

3 large peaches, halved and stoned

For the raspberry sauce

450g/1lb/2¹/2 cups fresh or
*   frozen raspberries*

15ml/1 tbsp lemon juice

25–40g/1–1¹/2oz/2–3 tbsp caster sugar

30–45ml/2–3 tbsp raspberry
*   liqueur (optional)*

vanilla ice cream, to serve

mint leaves, to decorate

COOK'S TIP

Prepare the peaches and sauce up to one day in advance. Leave the peaches in the syrup and cover them and the sauce before chilling.

In a large saucepan, combine the water, sugar and vanilla pod. Bring to the boil, stirring to dissolve the sugar. Add the peaches, cut-sides down, with water, if needed, to cover the fruit. Press a piece of greaseproof paper against the surface, then cover and simmer for 12–15 minutes until tender. Remove the pan from the heat and leave the peaches to cool. Peel the peaches.

Whiz the raspberries, lemon juice and sugar in a food processor for 1 minute, then sieve into a bowl. Add the raspberry liqueur, if using, and chill. To serve, place a peach half, cut-side up, add vanilla ice cream and spoon over the raspberry sauce. Decorate with mint leaves.

BLUEBERRY AND ORANGE SALAD WITH LAVENDER MERINGUES

Delicate blueberries and tangy oranges are combined with tiny lavender-flavoured meringues in this simple but stunning fruit salad. Lavender sprigs add the final decorative touch.

Serves 4

6 oranges
350g/12oz/3 cups blueberries
8 fresh lavender sprigs

For the meringue
2 egg whites
115g/4oz/½ cup caster sugar
5ml/1 tsp fresh lavender flowers

COOK'S TIP

Lavender is used in both sweet and savoury dishes. Always use fresh or recently dried flowers, and avoid artificially scented bunches that are sold for domestic purposes. Of course, if you can't find fresh lavender, then you could just make plain meringues instead.

Preheat the oven to 140°C/275°F/Gas 1. Line a baking tray with six layers of newspaper and cover with non-stick baking paper. Whisk the egg whites in a large mixing bowl until they hold soft peaks. Add the sugar a little at a time, whisking thoroughly after each addition until the meringue is thick and glossy, then fold in the lavender flowers.

Spoon the meringue into a piping bag fitted with a 5mm/¼in plain nozzle. Pipe as many small buttons of meringue on to the prepared baking sheet as you can. Bake the meringues near the bottom of the oven for 1½–2 hours.

To segment the oranges, remove the peel from the top, bottom and sides with a serrated knife. Loosen the segments by cutting with a paring knife between the flesh and the membranes, holding the fruit over a bowl, then arrange the segments on four plates.

Combine the blueberries with the lavender meringues and pile in the centre of each plate. Decorate with sprigs of lavender and serve.

SUMMER PUDDING

This is a classic English dessert, traditionally made in midsummer.

Serves 4

about 8 thin slices day-old white bread,
  crusts removed
750g/1¾lb/7 cups mixed berries
about 30ml/2 tbsp sugar

Cut a round from one slice of bread to fit in the base of a 1.2 litre/2 pint/ 5 cup pudding basin, then cut strips of bread about 5cm/2in wide to line the basin, overlapping the strips.

Gently heat the fruit, sugar and 30ml/2 tbsp water in a large heavy saucepan, shaking the pan occasionally, until the juices begin to run.

Reserve about 45ml/3 tbsp fruit juice, then spoon the fruit and remaining juice into the basin, taking care not to dislodge the bread.

Cut the remaining bread to fit entirely over the fruit. Stand the basin on a plate and cover with a saucer or small plate that will just fit inside the top of the basin. Place a heavy weight on top. Chill the pudding and the reserved fruit juice overnight. Run a knife around the inside of the basin, then invert the pudding on to a plate. Pour over the reserved juice and serve.

COOK'S TIP

Use a selection of soft, juicy berries such as redcurrants, raspberries and blackberries.

MIXED FRUIT AND BERRY SALAD WITH COFFEE CREAM

The inspiration for this refreshing sweet salad came from Japan. Scented fruits and berries are mixed together and served with minted coffee cream, which is excellent with fresh fruit.

Serves 6

1 small fresh pineapple

2 large ripe pears

2 fresh peaches

12 strawberries

12 canned lychees and the juice from
the can

6 small mint sprigs, plus extra sprigs
to decorate

15ml/1 tbsp instant coffee granules

30ml/2 tbsp boiling water

150ml/¼ pint/⅔ cup double cream

VARIATION

*Use fresh lychees when they are
in season. Choose fruit with a
pink or red skin which indicates
that the lychee will be sweet and
ripe. The skin is brittle and peels
off easily and the fruit should be
pearly white.*

Peel and stone the fruit as necessary and chop into even-size pieces. Place all the fruit in a large glass bowl and pour on the lychee juice. Chill for at least an hour until ready to serve.

To make the sauce, remove the leaves from the mint sprigs and place them in a food processor or blender with the instant coffee granules and boiling water. Blend until smooth. Add the cream and process again briefly.

Serve the fruit salad decorated with small sprigs of mint, and hand the coffee sauce round separately.

BLACKBERRY SALAD WITH ROSE GRANITA

Blackberries combine especially well with rose water. Here a rose syrup is frozen into a granita and served over strips of white meringue.

Serves 4

150g/5oz/²⁄₃ cup caster sugar

1 fresh red rose, petals finely chopped

5ml/1 tsp rose water

10ml/2 tsp lemon juice

450g/1lb/4 cups blackberries

icing sugar, for dusting

For the meringue

2 egg whites

115g/4oz/¹⁄₂ cup caster sugar

COOK'S TIP

Blackberries are widely cultivated from late spring to autumn and are usually juicy, plump and sweet. The finest berries have a slightly bitter edge and a strong depth of flavour. They are best appreciated with a light sprinkling of sugar.

Bring 150ml/¼ pint/²⁄₃ cup water to the boil in a stainless-steel or enamel saucepan. Add the sugar and rose petals, then simmer for 5 minutes. Strain the syrup into a deep metal tray, add a further 450ml/¾ pint/scant 1⁷⁄₈ cups water, the rose water and lemon juice, and leave to cool. Freeze the mixture for 3 hours or until solid.

Preheat the oven to 140°C/275°F/Gas 1. Line a baking sheet with six layers of newspaper and cover with non-stick baking paper.

To make the meringue, whisk the egg whites until they hold soft peaks. Add the caster sugar a little at a time and whisk until firm.

Spoon the meringue into a piping bag fitted with a 1cm/¹⁄₂in plain nozzle. Pipe the meringue in lengths across the paper-lined baking sheet. Bake in the bottom of the oven for 1¹⁄₂–2 hours.

Break the meringue into 5cm/2in lengths and place three or four lengths on each of four large plates. Pile the blackberries next to the meringue. With a tablespoon, scrape the granita finely. Shape into ovals and place over the meringue. Dust with icing sugar and serve.

STRAWBERRIES WITH RASPBERRY AND PASSION FRUIT SAUCE

Strawberries release their finest flavour when served with raspberry and passion fruit sauce.

Serves 4

350g/12oz/2 cups raspberries, fresh or frozen

45ml/3 tbsp caster sugar

2 passion fruits

700g/1¹/₂lb/4 cups small strawberries

8 plain finger biscuits, to serve

Place the raspberries and sugar in a saucepan and cook over a low heat, stirring occasionally, until simmering. Cook gently for 5 minutes, then leave to cool. Halve the passion fruits and scoop out the seeds and juice. Pour the raspberries into a blender or food processor, add the passion fruit pulp and blend for a few seconds.

Rub the fruit sauce through a fine nylon sieve to remove the seeds. Fold the strawberries into the sauce, then spoon into four stemmed glasses. Serve with plain finger biscuits.

COOK'S TIP

When buying strawberries, choose fruit that is brightly coloured, firm and unblemished. For the best flavour, serve the berries at room temperature. The delicate flavour will then be at its most intense.

FROZEN RASPBERRY MOUSSE

This dessert is like a frozen soufflé. Freeze it in a ring mould, then you can fill the centre with fresh raspberries moistened with crème de framboise or raspberry liqueur or just a little orange juice.

Serves 6

350g/12oz/2 cups raspberries, plus more for serving

45ml/3 tbsp icing sugar

2 egg whites

1.5ml/¼ tsp cream of tartar

90g/3½oz/½ cup granulated sugar

25ml/1½ tbsp lemon juice

250ml/8fl oz/1 cup whipping cream

15ml/1 tbsp crème de framboise or Kirsch

mint leaves, to decorate

Purée the raspberries in a food processor, then sieve. Pour a third of the purée into a bowl, stir in the icing sugar, cover and chill. Reserve the remaining purée. Whisk the egg whites, cream of tartar, sugar and lemon juice in a heatproof bowl over a pan of simmering water until stiffly peaking. Remove the bowl from the pan and continue beating for 2–3 minutes until cool. Fold in the reserved raspberry purée. Whip the cream until it forms soft peaks and fold into the raspberry mixture with the liqueur. Spoon into a 1.5 litre/2½ pint/6¼ cup ring mould, cover and freeze overnight. To unmould, dip the mould in warm water for about 5 seconds and wipe the base. Invert a plate over the mould and, holding them tightly, turn over together, then lift off the mould. Fill the mousse centre with raspberries, decorate with mint leaves and serve with the raspberry purée.

RASPBERRY SALAD WITH MANGO CUSTARD SAUCE

This attractive salad unites the sharp quality of fresh raspberries and fragrant mango with two special sauces made from the same fruits.

Serves 4

1 large mango

3 egg yolks

30ml/2 tbsp caster sugar

10ml/2 tsp cornflour

200ml/7fl oz/scant 1 cup milk

8 fresh mint sprigs, to decorate

For the raspberry sauce

500g/1¼lb/3⅓ cups raspberries

45ml/3 tbsp caster sugar

COOK'S TIP

Mangoes are ripe when they yield to gentle pressure in the hand. Some varieties show a red-gold or yellow flush when they are ready to eat.

To prepare the mango, remove the top and bottom with a serrated knife. Cut away the outer skin, then remove the flesh by cutting either side of the flat central stone. Save one half of the fruit for decoration and roughly chop the rest of the flesh.

To make the custard, combine the egg yolks, sugar, cornflour and 30ml/2 tbsp of the milk smoothly in a bowl.

Rinse out a small saucepan with cold water to prevent the milk from catching. Bring the rest of the milk to the boil in the pan, pour it over the egg yolk mixture in the bowl and stir evenly.

Strain the mixture back into the saucepan. Cook over a low heat, stirring constantly, until it thickens enough to coat the back of the spoon.

Pour the custard into a food processor or blender, add the chopped mango and blend until smooth. Leave to cool.

To make the raspberry sauce, place 350g/12oz/2 cups of the raspberries in a stainless-steel saucepan. Add the sugar, soften over a gentle heat and simmer for 5 minutes. Using a wooden spoon, rub the fruit through a fine nylon sieve to remove the seeds. Leave to cool.

Spoon the raspberry sauce and mango custard into two pools on four plates. Slice the reserved mango and fan out or arrange in a pattern over the raspberry sauce. Scatter fresh raspberries over the mango custard. Decorate with mint sprigs and serve.

RASPBERRY AND PASSION FRUIT SWIRLS

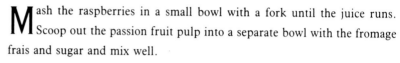

If passion fruits are not available, this simple low-fat dessert can be made with raspberries alone.

Serves 4

300g/11oz/scant 2 cups raspberries

2 passion fruits

400g/14oz/1⅔ cups low-fat
* fromage frais*

30ml/2 tbsp caster sugar

raspberries and mint sprigs, to decorate

Mash the raspberries in a small bowl with a fork until the juice runs. Scoop out the passion fruit pulp into a separate bowl with the fromage frais and sugar and mix well.

Spoon alternate spoonfuls of the raspberry pulp and the fromage frais mixture into stemmed glasses or one large serving dish, stirring lightly to create a swirled effect.

Decorate each dessert with a whole raspberry and a fresh mint sprig. Chill until ready to serve.

COOK'S TIP

Over-ripe, slightly soft fruit can also be used in this recipe. Use frozen raspberries when fresh are not available, but thaw them first.

APPLE FOAM WITH BLACKBERRIES

Any seasonal soft fruit can be used for this delicious dessert if blackberries are not available at the time.

Serves 4

225g/8oz/2 cups blackberries
150ml/¼ pint/⅔ cup apple juice
5ml/1 tsp powdered gelatine
15ml/1 tbsp clear honey
2 egg whites

COOK'S TIP
Make sure that you add the gelatine to a cold liquid before dissolving over a very low heat. Gelatine must not boil, or it will lose its setting ability. Once set, gelatine mixtures should be left in the fridge for about 2 hours to become firm. Don't be tempted to chill a gelatine mixture quickly in the freezer, as it tends to crystallize and separate.

Place the blackberries in a pan with 60ml/4 tbsp of the apple juice and heat gently until the fruit is soft. Remove from the heat, cool and chill.

Sprinkle the gelatine over the remaining apple juice in a small pan and stir over a low heat until dissolved. Stir in the honey.

Whisk the egg whites until they hold stiff peaks. Continue whisking hard and pour in the hot gelatine mixture gradually, until well mixed.

Quickly spoon the foam into rough mounds on individual plates. Chill. Serve with the blackberries and juice spooned around.

FRESH RASPBERRY AND PASSION FRUIT CHINCHILLA SOUFFLES

Few desserts are as easy to make as this one: beaten egg whites and sugar, combined with passion fruits, are baked in a dish, turned out and served with a handful of raspberries.

Serves 4

25g/1oz/2 tbsp butter, softened

5 egg whites

150g/5oz/²⁄₃ cup caster sugar

2 passion fruits

250ml/8fl oz/1 cup ready-made custard from a carton or can

milk, as required

675g/1¹⁄₂lb/4 cups fresh raspberries

icing sugar, for dusting

Preheat the oven to 180°C/350°F/Gas 4. Brush four 300ml/½ pint/1¼ cup soufflé dishes with a visible layer of soft butter.

Whisk the egg whites in a mixing bowl until firm. (You can use an electric whisk.) Add the sugar a little at a time and whisk into a firm meringue.

Halve the passion fruits, take out the seeds with a spoon and fold them into the meringue.

Spoon the meringue into the prepared dishes, stand in a deep roasting tin which has been half-filled with boiling water and bake for 10 minutes. The meringue will rise above the tops of the soufflé dishes.

Turn the chinchillas out upside-down on to serving plates. Thin the custard with a little milk and pour around the edge.

Top with raspberries, dredge with icing sugar and serve warm or cold.

VARIATION

If raspberries are out of season, use either fresh, bottled or canned soft fruit such as strawberries, blueberries, blackberries or redcurrants.

FIG AND PEAR COMPOTE WITH RASPBERRIES

A simple yet sophisticated dessert featuring succulent, ripe autumnal fruits, enhanced by tangy raspberries.

Serves 4

75g/3oz/6 tbsp caster sugar

1 bottle red wine

1 vanilla pod, split

1 strip pared lemon rind

4 pears

2 purple figs, quartered

225g/8oz/1 1/3 cups fresh raspberries

lemon juice, to taste

Put the sugar and wine in a large pan and heat gently until dissolved. Add the vanilla pod and lemon rind and bring to the boil. Simmer for 5 minutes. Peel and halve the pears, then scoop out the cores, using a melon baller. Add the pears to the syrup and poach for 15 minutes, turning the pears several times so they colour evenly. Add the figs and poach for a further 5 minutes, until the fruits are tender. Transfer the poached fruit to a serving bowl using a slotted spoon, then scatter over the raspberries.

Return the syrup to the heat and boil rapidly to reduce slightly. Add a little lemon juice to taste. Strain over the fruits and serve warm.

ICED PINEAPPLE CRUSH WITH STRAWBERRIES AND LYCHEES

The sweet tropical flavours of pineapple and lychees mixed with strawberries make this a refreshing salad.

Serves 4

2 small pineapples

450g/1lb/3 cups strawberries

400g/14oz can lychees

45ml/3 tbsp Kirsch or white rum

30ml/2 tbsp icing sugar

COOK'S TIP

A ripe pineapple will resist pressure when squeezed and will have a sweet, fragrant smell. In winter, freezing conditions can cause the flesh to blacken.

Remove the crown from both pineapples by twisting sharply. Reserve the leaves for decoration. Cut the fruit in half diagonally with a large serrated knife. Cut around the flesh inside the skin with a small serrated knife, keeping the skin intact. Remove the core from the pineapple.

Chop the pineapple and combine with the strawberries and lychees, taking care not to damage the fruit. Combine the Kirsch or white rum with the icing sugar, pour over the fruit and freeze for 45 minutes. Spoon the semi-frozen fruit into the pineapple skins and decorate with pineapple leaves.

Pastries and Pies

Berries, either alone or with other fruits, make brilliant

fillings for pies and tarts. Their soft, juicy texture

makes a mouth-watering combination with flaky pastry

or feather-light sponge.

RED BERRY SPONGE TART

Use a selection of berries for this delicious sponge tart. Serve warm from the oven with vanilla ice cream.

Serves 4

softened butter, for greasing

450g/1lb/3 cups soft berry fruits, such
*   as raspberries, blackberries,*
*   blackcurrants, redcurrants,*
*   strawberries or blueberries*

2 eggs, at room temperature

50g/2oz/¼ cup caster sugar, plus extra
*   to taste (optional)*

15ml/1 tbsp plain flour

50g/2oz/¾ cup ground almonds

vanilla ice cream, to serve

VARIATION

When berry fruits are out of
season, use thawed frozen fruits,
or alternatively use bottled
fruits, but ensure that they are
well drained before use.

Preheat the oven to 190°C/375°F/Gas 5. Brush the base and sides of a 23cm/9in flan tin with softened butter and line the base with a circle of non-stick baking paper. Scatter the fruits in the tin with a little sugar, to taste, if the fruits are tart.

Whisk the eggs and sugar together for about 3–4 minutes or until they leave a thick trail across the surface. Combine the flour and almonds, then fold into the egg mixture with a spatula – retaining as much air as possible.

Spread the mixture on top of the fruit base and bake in the oven for 15 minutes. Transfer to a serving plate and serve with vanilla ice cream.

BLUEBERRY AND PEAR PIE

The combination of blueberries and pears makes a sweet and juicy pie. Serve warm with crème fraîche or try a scoop or two of vanilla ice cream.

Serves 4

225g/8oz/2 cups plain flour
pinch of salt
50g/2oz/4 tbsp lard, cubed
50g/2oz/4 tbsp butter, cubed
675g/1¹/₂lb/6 cups blueberries
30ml/2 tbsp caster sugar
15ml/1 tbsp arrowroot
2 ripe, but firm pears, peeled, cored
  and sliced
2.5ml/¹/₂ tsp ground cinnamon
grated rind of ¹/₂ lemon
beaten egg, to glaze
caster sugar, for sprinkling
crème fraîche, to serve

Sift the flour and salt into a bowl and rub in the lard and butter until the mixture resembles fine breadcrumbs. Stir in 45ml/3 tbsp cold water and mix to a dough. Chill for 30 minutes.

Place 225g/8oz/2 cups of the blueberries in a pan with the sugar. Cover and cook gently until the berries are soft. Press through a nylon sieve.

Blend the arrowroot with 30ml/2 tbsp cold water and add to the blueberry purée. Bring to the boil, stirring until thickened. Cool slightly.

Place a baking sheet in the oven and preheat to 190°C/375°F/Gas 5. Roll out just over half the pastry on a lightly floured surface and use to line a 20cm/8in shallow pie dish or plate.

Mix together the remaining blueberries, the pears, cinnamon and lemon rind and spoon into the dish. Pour over the blueberry purée.

Roll out the remaining pastry and use to cover the pie. Make a small slit in the centre. Brush with egg and sprinkle with sugar. Bake on the hot baking sheet, for 40–45 minutes, until golden. Serve warm with crème fraîche.

STRAWBERRY AND BLUEBERRY PIE

This tart works equally well using any combination of berries that are available, as long as there is a riot of colour and the fruit is in perfect condition.

Serves 6–8
225g/8oz/2 cups plain flour
pinch of salt
75g/3oz/9 tbsp icing sugar
150g/5oz/10 tbsp unsalted butter, diced
1 egg yolk

For the filling
350g/12oz/1¼ cups mascarpone cheese
30ml/2 tbsp icing sugar
few drops vanilla essence
finely grated rind of 1 orange
450–675g/1–1½lb/3–5 cups fresh
  mixed strawberries and blueberries
90ml/6 tbsp redcurrant jelly
30ml/2 tbsp orange juice

Sift the flour, salt and sugar into a bowl, and rub in the butter until the mixture resembles coarse crumbs. Using a round-bladed knife, mix in the egg yolk and 10ml/2 tsp cold water. Gather the dough together, then turn out on to a floured surface and knead lightly until smooth. Wrap in clear film and chill in the fridge for 1 hour.

Preheat the oven to 190°C/375°F/Gas 5. Roll out the pastry and use to line a 25cm/10in fluted flan tin. Prick the base and chill for 15 minutes.

Line the chilled pastry case with greaseproof paper and baking beans, then bake for 15 minutes. Remove the paper and beans and bake for a further 15 minutes, until crisp and golden. Leave to cool in the tin.

Beat together the mascarpone, sugar, vanilla essence and orange rind in a mixing bowl until the mixture is smooth.

Remove the pastry case from the tin, then spoon in the filling and pile the fruits on top. Heat the redcurrant jelly with the orange juice until runny, sieve if necessary, then brush over the fruit to glaze.

RED BERRY TART WITH LEMON CREAM FILLING

Just right for warm summer days, this flan is best filled just before serving so the pastry remains mouth-wateringly crisp. Select red berries such as strawberries, raspberries or redcurrants.

Serves 6–8
150g/5oz/1¼ cups plain flour
25g/1oz/¼ cup cornflour
30g/1½oz/3 tbsp icing sugar
100g/3½oz/8 tbsp butter
5ml/1 tsp vanilla essence
2 egg yolks, beaten

For the filling
200g/7oz/scant 1 cup cream
  cheese, softened
45ml/3 tbsp lemon curd
grated rind and juice of 1 lemon
icing sugar, to sweeten (optional)
225g/8oz/1½ cups mixed red
  berry fruits
45ml/3 tbsp redcurrant jelly

VARIATION
Leave out the redcurrant jelly and sprinkle with icing sugar.

Sift the flour, cornflour and icing sugar together, then rub in the butter until the mixture resembles breadcrumbs.

Beat the vanilla into the egg yolks, then mix into the crumbs to make a firm dough, adding cold water if necessary.

Roll out and line a 23cm/9in round flan tin, pressing the dough well up the sides after trimming. Prick the base of the flan with a fork and leave to rest in the fridge for 30 minutes.

Preheat the oven to 200°C/400°F/Gas 6. Line the flan with greaseproof paper and baking beans. Place the tin on a baking sheet and bake for 20 minutes, removing the paper and beans for the last 5 minutes. When cooked, cool and remove the pastry case from the flan tin.

Cream the cheese, lemon curd and lemon rind and juice, adding icing sugar to sweeten, if you wish. Spread the mixture into the base of the flan.

Top the flan with the fruits. Warm the redcurrant jelly and trickle it over the fruits just before serving.

Meringues and Gâteaux

Rich red and black berries, combined with cream or

yogurt, make delectable fillings and terrific toppings

for melt-in-the-mouth meringues, gorgeous gâteaux and

crisp summer shortcakes.

RASPBERRY AND NECTARINE PAVLOVA

This meringue cake was created in the 1920s for the ballerina Anna Pavlova, when she visited Australia.

Serves 4–6

3 egg whites

175g/6oz/3/4 cup caster sugar

5ml/1 tsp cornflour

5ml/1 tsp white wine vinegar

40g/1½oz/5 tbsp chopped
   roasted hazelnuts

250ml/8fl oz/1 cup double cream

15ml/1 tbsp orange juice

30ml/2 tbsp natural thick and
   creamy yogurt

2 ripe nectarines, stoned and sliced

225g/8oz/1⅓ cups raspberries, halved

15–30ml/1–2 tbsp redcurrant
   jelly, warmed

Preheat the oven to 140°C/275°F/Gas 1. Lightly grease a baking sheet. Draw a 20cm/8in circle on a sheet of non-stick baking paper. Place pencil-side down on the baking sheet.

Put the egg whites in a clean, grease-free bowl and whisk with an electric mixer until stiff. Whisk in the sugar, 15ml/1 tbsp at a time, whisking well after each addition. Add the cornflour, vinegar and hazelnuts and fold in carefully with a large metal spoon. Spoon the meringue on to the marked circle and spread out to the edges, making a dip in the centre. Bake for about 1¼–1½ hours, until crisp. Leave to cool completely and transfer to a serving platter. Whip the cream and orange juice until just thick, stir in the yogurt and spoon on to the meringue. Top with the fruit and drizzle over the redcurrant jelly. Serve immediately.

BLACKBERRY BROWN SUGAR MERINGUE

Brown sugar gives this meringue a delicate, fudge-like flavour which combines well with the berry filling.

Serves 6

175g/6oz/1 cup soft light brown sugar

3 egg whites

5ml/1 tsp distilled malt vinegar

2.5ml/½ tsp vanilla essence

For the filling

350–450g/12oz–1lb/3–4 cups
  blackberries

30ml/2 tbsp crème de cassis

300ml/½ pint/1¼ cups double cream

15ml/1 tbsp icing sugar, sifted

small blackberry leaves, to
  decorate (optional)

Preheat the oven to 160°C/325°F/Gas 3. Draw a 20cm/8in circle on a sheet of non-stick baking paper, turn over and place on a baking sheet.

Spread out the brown sugar on another baking sheet and dry in the oven for 8–10 minutes. Sieve to remove any lumps.

Whisk the egg whites in a bowl until stiff. Add half the dried brown sugar, 15ml/1 tbsp at a time, whisking well after each addition. Add the vinegar and vanilla essence, then fold in the remaining sugar.

Spoon the meringue on to the drawn circle on the paper, making a hollow in the centre. Bake for 45 minutes, then turn off the oven and leave the meringue in the oven with the door slightly open, until cold.

Place the blackberries in a bowl, sprinkle over the crème de cassis and leave to macerate for 30 minutes.

When the meringue is cold, carefully peel off the non-stick baking paper and transfer the meringue to a serving plate. Lightly whip the cream with the icing sugar and spoon into the centre. Top with the blackberries and decorate with small blackberry leaves, if liked. Serve at once.

RASPBERRY MERINGUE GATEAU

A crisp, rich, hazelnut meringue filled with whipped cream and raspberries makes a wonderful dessert served with a fresh raspberry and orange sauce.

Serves 6

4 egg whites

225g/8oz/1 cup caster sugar

few drops vanilla essence

5ml/1 tsp distilled malt vinegar

115g/4oz/1 cup roasted and chopped
*   hazelnuts, ground*

300ml/½ pint/1¼ cups double cream

350g/12oz/2 cups raspberries

icing sugar, for dusting

raspberries and mint sprigs, to decorate

For the sauce

225g/8oz/1⅓ cups raspberries

45–60ml/3–4 tbsp icing sugar, sifted

15ml/1 tbsp orange liqueur

Preheat the oven to 180°C/350°F/Gas 4. Grease two 20cm/8in sandwich tins and line the bases with greaseproof paper.

Whisk the egg whites in a large bowl until they hold stiff peaks, then gradually whisk in the caster sugar a tablespoon at a time, whisking well after each addition to create a smooth mixture.

Continue whisking the meringue mixture for a minute or two until very stiff, then fold in the vanilla essence, vinegar and ground hazelnuts.

Divide the meringue mixture between the prepared sandwich tins and spread level. Bake for 50–60 minutes, until crisp. Remove the meringues from the tins and leave to cool on a wire rack.

While the meringues are cooling, make the sauce. Purée the raspberries with the icing sugar and orange liqueur in a blender or food processor, then press the purée through a fine nylon sieve to remove any pips. Chill the sauce until ready to serve.

Whip the cream until it forms soft peaks, then gently fold in the raspberries. Sandwich the meringue rounds together with the raspberry cream. Dust the top of the gâteau with icing sugar. Decorate with raspberries and mint sprigs and serve with the raspberry sauce.

VARIATION

Fresh redcurrants make a good alternative to raspberries. Add to the cream with a little sugar.

SUMMER STRAWBERRY GATEAU

No one could resist the appeal of little heartsease pansies. This strawberry-filled cake would be lovely for a summer occasion in the garden.

Serves 6–8

100g/3¾oz/scant ½ cup soft margarine
100g/3¾oz/scant ½ cup caster sugar
10ml/2 tsp clear honey
150g/5oz/1¼ cups self-raising flour
2.5ml/½ tsp baking powder
30ml/2 tbsp milk
2 eggs, plus 1 egg white for crystallizing
15ml/1 tbsp rose water
15ml/1 tbsp Cointreau or
  orange liqueur
16 heartsease pansy flowers
caster sugar, for crystallizing
icing sugar, to decorate
450g/1lb/3 cups strawberries
strawberry leaves, to decorate

Preheat the oven to 190°C/375°F/Gas 5. Grease and lightly flour a ring mould. Put the soft margarine, sugar, honey, flour, baking powder, milk and 2 eggs into a mixing bowl and beat well for 1 minute. Add the rose water and Cointreau or orange liqueur and mix well.

Pour the mixture into the prepared tin and bake for 40 minutes, or until a skewer inserted in the centre comes out clean. Leave to stand for a few minutes and then turn out on to a wire rack and leave to cool.

Crystallize the pansies by painting them with lightly beaten egg white and sprinkling lightly with caster sugar. Leave to dry.

Transfer the cake to a serving plate and sift over a little icing sugar. Fill the centre of the ring with strawberries and decorate with crystallized pansies and strawberry leaves.

AMERICAN BERRY SHORTCAKE

This classic dessert can be assembled up to an hour in advance and kept chilled until required.

Serves 8

300ml/¹/₂ pint/1¹/₄ cups
  whipping cream
25g/1oz/2 tbsp icing sugar, sifted
675g/1¹/₂lb/4 cups strawberries or
  mixed berries, halved or sliced if large
50g/2oz/¹/₄ cup caster sugar, or to taste

For the shortcake

225g/8oz/2 cups plain flour
10ml/2 tsp baking powder
65g/2¹/₂oz/5 tbsp caster sugar
115g/4oz/¹/₂ cup butter
75ml/5 tbsp milk
1 size 1 egg

Preheat the oven to 230°C/450°F/Gas 8. Grease a 20cm/8in round cake tin. To make the shortcake, sift the flour, baking powder and sugar into a bowl. Add the butter and rub in until the mixture resembles fine crumbs. Combine the milk and egg. Add to the crumb mixture and stir just until evenly mixed to a soft dough.

Put the dough in the prepared tin and pat out to an even layer. Bake for 15–20 minutes or until a wooden skewer inserted in the centre comes out clean. Leave to cool slightly.

Whip the cream until it starts to thicken. Add the icing sugar and continue whipping until the cream will hold soft peaks.

Put the berries in a bowl. Sprinkle with the caster sugar and toss together lightly. Cover and set aside for the berries to give up some juice.

Remove the cooled shortcake from the tin. With a long, serrated knife, split the shortcake horizontally into two equal layers.

Put the bottom layer on a serving plate. Top with half of the berries and most of the cream. Set the second layer on top and press down gently. Spoon the remaining berries over the top layer (or serve them separately) and add the remaining cream in small, decorative dollops.

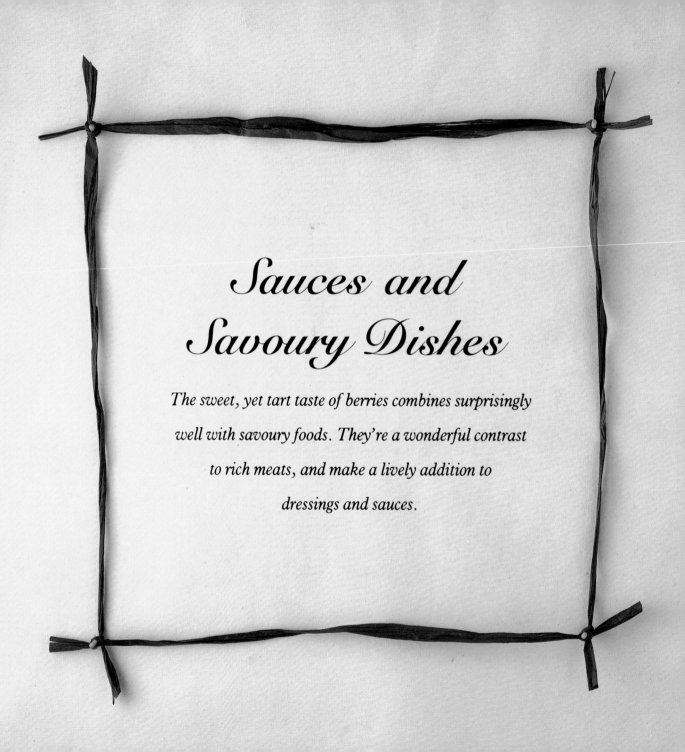

Sauces and Savoury Dishes

The sweet, yet tart taste of berries combines surprisingly

well with savoury foods. They're a wonderful contrast

to rich meats, and make a lively addition to

dressings and sauces.

ASPARAGUS WITH CREAMY RASPBERRY VINAIGRETTE

This simple starter is an unusual and delicious way to serve the first raspberries of the summer.

Serves 4

675g/1½lb thin asparagus spears
30ml/2 tbsp raspberry vinegar
2.5ml/½ tsp salt
5ml/1 tsp Dijon mustard
75ml/5 tbsp sunflower oil
30ml/2 tbsp soured cream or
   plain yogurt
white pepper
175g/6oz/1 cup fresh raspberries

Fill a large wide pan or wok with 10cm/4in water and bring to the boil. Trim the ends of the asparagus spears. If desired, remove the "scales" using a vegetable peeler. Tie the asparagus into two bundles. Lower the bundles into the boiling water and cook for 2 minutes, until just tender.

With a slotted spoon, carefully remove the asparagus bundles from the boiling water and immerse in cold water to stop the cooking. Drain and untie the bundles. Pat dry with kitchen paper. Chill the asparagus at least 1 hour.

Put the vinegar and salt in a bowl and stir with a fork until dissolved. Stir in the mustard, then gradually stir in the oil until blended. Add the soured cream or yogurt and pepper to taste.

To serve, place the asparagus on individual plates and drizzle the dressing across the middle of the spears. Garnish with the fresh raspberries.

STIR-FRIED DUCK WITH BLUEBERRIES

Serve this conveniently quick dinner party dish with fresh mint sprigs, which will give a wonderful fresh aroma as you bring the meal to the table.

Serves 4

2 duck breasts, about 175g/6oz each

30ml/2 tbsp sunflower oil

15ml/1 tbsp red wine vinegar

5ml/1 tsp sugar

5ml/1 tsp red wine

5ml/1 tsp crème de cassis

115g/4oz/1 cup fresh blueberries

15ml/1 tbsp chopped fresh mint

salt and ground black pepper

fresh mint sprigs, to garnish

Cut the duck breasts crossways into thin slices. Season well with salt and ground black pepper.

Heat a wok or large frying pan and add the oil. When the oil is hot, stir-fry the duck for 3 minutes.

Add the red wine vinegar, sugar, red wine and crème de cassis. Bubble for 3 minutes, to reduce to a thick syrup.

Stir in the blueberries, sprinkle over the chopped mint and then serve garnished with fresh mint sprigs.

CHICKEN STEW WITH BLACKBERRIES AND LEMON BALM

The combination of red wine and blackberries in this delicious stew gives it a dramatic appearance.

Serves 4

4 chicken breasts, partly boned

25g/1oz/2 tbsp butter

15ml/1 tbsp sunflower oil

25g/1oz/4 tbsp flour

150ml/¼ pint/⅔ cup red wine

150ml/¼ pint/⅔ cup chicken stock

grated rind of ½ orange plus
*   15ml/1 tbsp juice*

2 lemon balm sprigs, finely chopped,
*   plus a few extra sprigs to garnish*

150ml/¼ pint/⅔ cup double cream

1 egg yolk

salt and ground black pepper

100g/4oz/⅔ cup fresh blackberries,
*   plus 50g/2oz/⅓ cup to garnish*

Remove any skin from the chicken, and season the meat. Heat the butter and oil in a pan, fry the chicken to seal it, then transfer to a casserole. Stir the flour into the pan, then add wine and stock and bring to the boil. Add the orange rind and juice, and the lemon balm. Pour over the chicken.

Preheat the oven to 180°C/350°F/Gas 4. Cover the casserole and cook in the oven for about 40 minutes.

Blend the cream with the egg yolk, add some of the liquid from the casserole and stir back into the dish with the blackberries. Cover and cook for a further 10–15 minutes. Serve garnished with the rest of the blackberries and lemon balm sprigs.

VENISON WITH CRANBERRY SAUCE

Venison steaks are now readily available. Lean and low in fat, they are the healthy choice for a special occasion. Served with a sauce of fresh seasonal cranberries, port and ginger, they make a delicious dish with a wonderful combination of flavours.

Serves 4

1 orange

1 lemon

75g/3oz/³⁄₄ cup fresh or frozen
*   cranberries*

5ml/1 tsp grated fresh root ginger

1 thyme sprig

5ml/1 tsp Dijon mustard

60ml/4 tbsp redcurrant jelly

150ml/¹⁄₄ pint/²⁄₃ cup ruby port

30ml/2 tbsp sunflower oil

4 venison steaks

2 shallots, finely chopped

salt and ground black pepper

thyme sprigs, to garnish

creamy mashed potatoes and broccoli,
*   to serve*

Pare the rind from half the orange and half the lemon using a vegetable peeler, then cut into very fine strips.

Blanch the strips in a small pan of boiling water for about 5 minutes until tender. Drain the strips and refresh under cold water.

Squeeze the juice from the orange and lemon and then pour into a small pan. Add the fresh or frozen cranberries, ginger, thyme sprig, mustard, redcurrant jelly and port. Cook over a low heat until the jelly melts.

Bring the sauce to the boil, stirring occasionally, then cover the pan and reduce the heat. Continue to cook gently, for about 15 minutes, until the cranberries are just tender.

Heat the oil in a heavy-based frying pan, add the venison steaks and cook over a high heat for 2–3 minutes.

Turn over the steaks and add the shallots to the pan. Cook the steaks on the other side for 2–3 minutes, depending on whether you like rare or medium-cooked meat.

Just before the end of cooking, pour in the sauce and add the strips of orange and lemon rind to the pan. Leave the sauce to bubble for a few seconds to thicken slightly, then remove the thyme sprig and adjust the seasoning to taste.

Transfer the venison steaks to warmed plates and spoon over the sauce. Garnish with thyme sprigs and serve accompanied by creamy mashed potatoes and broccoli.

FRESH BERRY SALSA

This bright, tangy salsa is spicy hot – add more chilli if you would like to make it even more fiery. It is good served with grilled chicken or fish.

Serves 4–6

1 fresh chilli

½ red onion, minced

2 spring onions, chopped

1 tomato, finely diced

1 small yellow pepper, seeded and finely chopped

10g/¼oz/¼ cup chopped fresh coriander

1.5ml/¼ tsp salt

15ml/1 tbsp raspberry vinegar

15ml/1 tbsp fresh orange juice

5ml/1 tsp honey

15ml/1 tbsp olive oil

150g/5oz/1 cup strawberries

115g/4oz/1 cup blueberries or blackberries

175g/6oz/1 cup raspberries

Finely chop the chilli (discard the seeds and membrane if a less hot flavour is desired) and place in a large bowl.

Add the red onion, spring onions, tomato, pepper, and coriander and stir together to blend well.

To make the dressing, whisk together the salt, vinegar, orange juice, honey and oil in a small bowl. Pour over the chilli mixture and stir well.

Hull the strawberries, rinse and pat dry if necessary. Coarsely chop the strawberries, then add to the chilli mixture with the blueberries or blackberries and raspberries, and stir to blend. Leave the mixture to stand at room temperature for 3 hours or until required.

Serve the salsa at room temperature.

INDEX